GET EIGHT REFERRALS OR MORE NOW

Obtain Them, Most of the Time, From Every Prospect or Client/Customer

REUVEN SHUVAL

Reuven Shuval Publisher
Hillsboro, OR, USA

Copyright © 2014 by Reuven Shuval
No part of this book may be reproduced, stored in a retrieval system, or transmitted in any form. Reproduction by electronic, mechanical, photocopying, recorded means or otherwise without prior written permission from Reuven Shuval is strictly forbidden.

All rights reserved.

ISBN-13: 978-1494873073
ISBN-10: 1494873079

To inquire about the availability of the author, Reuven Shuval, for speaking engagements or receiving significant discounts for bulk sales, please contact Reuven Shuval at Reuven@eightreferrals.com or phone (503) 939-4903.

DEDICATION

This book is dedicated to all the tens of millions of small businesses and salespeople who desire to be more successful and profitable.

CONTENTS

For Skeptics Only — vii

Chapter 1: Where Is the Beef? — 1

Chapter 2: Paradigm Shift — 7

Chapter 3: Psychological Barriers — 15

Chapter 4: The Initial Positioning — 23

Chapter 5: The Referral Conversation — 27

Chapter 6: Easier to Get Started — 47

Appendix I — 55

Appendix II — 57

About the Author — 61

FOR SKEPTICS ONLY

You have just read the book's title, "Get Eight Referrals or More Now: Obtain Them, Most of the Time, from Every Prospect or Client/Customer," and you are wondering, could it really be possible and doable?

The answer is absolutely YES. But it absolutely will *not* work if you follow acceptable and traditional ways of getting referrals.

It will only work if you follow the steps, the dialogues, and the rationale outlined in this book. This strategy mostly goes *against* conventional wisdom that the majority of people follows and accepts, and that is why it works.

You will not find this strategy on the web, by reading marketing and referral books, or by listening to referral gurus and other marketing experts.

You will also be pleasantly surprised to discover how easy the strategy is. It is not complicated and can be implemented immediately after you read the book.

Some of you may be wondering how I ever figured out this strategy that you are about to discover in the next chapters. Well, it was not easy. It took me a long time to figure it out and perfect it.

The breakthrough came when I started thinking outside the box and questioning traditional knowledge. I realized that conventional wisdom was not working and will never work in getting referrals the way I envisioned was possible. (More about that in the next chapters.)

So if you read this book and implement the strategy fully, not only will you have an amazing referral machine but also a great business. I'd be surprised if your return on investment wasn't at least a thousand times the price of the book.

Bottom line: referrals are too important to be left to chance. Have a simple strategy that works in getting eight or more referrals, most of the time, from every prospect or client/customer.

1
WHERE IS THE BEEF?

In 1984, Wendy's debuted its now iconic "Where's the Beef?" commercial starring Clara Peller as an old lady demanding more meat from her fast-food hamburger. The catchphrase was a sharp jab at competitors Burger King and McDonald's. The ad was credited with boosting Wendy's annual revenue by a whopping 31 percent. Three decades later, "Where's the Beef?" lives on as one of the greatest television commercials of all time.

"Where the beef?" is a question I asked myself for the past three decades as a small-business owner and a salesman regarding referral advice I got from books, experts, and other sources.

Over the years, I read many marketing books about referrals, heard the top experts in the field, went to seminars, and purchased tapes and DVDs. But I always felt something was missing. I asked repeatedly: "Where's the beef?"

WHERE IS THE BEEF?

What was missing, and what I have to offer you in this book, is a proven, simple, workable referral strategy that is also *quantifiable*. One that costs you nothing, is not complex, is not time-consuming, can be implemented immediately, and produces results almost every time.

No other referral system or method—at least none I've ever heard or read of—gives you the outcome (or even close to it) of this system.

As most of you know, referrals are the Holy Grail of marketing. Nothing beats them. Nothing!

So let's go over the tremendous benefits you and your business will have by implementing the very easy referral strategy outlined in this book:

- Referrals cost you almost nothing to acquire.

- Your sales will often be larger and easier.

- Price will be less of an issue.

- Your whole sale process will move faster, and your closing ratio will be much higher.

- You will stop getting only a few referrals that are based on luck or hit-and-miss requests.

- You will have an easy workable strategy to get referrals continuously.

- You will substantially lower your fear of asking for referrals. (You might even start enjoying it.)

- You will have peace of mind in knowing you have a steady flow of new, quality prospects.

- You will be able to build and expand your business much faster.

- You will stop throwing too many hard earned dollars into marketing programs that do not produce results.

- You will reduce the ups and downs of your feast-and-famine income cycle.

To get the most out of this book, let me first say that I believe quality is better than quantity. Less is sometimes more. Therefore, I kept the book short and only included what you need to know to implement the referral strategy.

The strategy, again, is getting eight referrals or more and obtaining them, most of the time, from *every* prospect or client/customer—and doing it as soon as possible.

Second, I believe your time is valuable, so the sooner you get through this book, the faster you and your business can enjoy all the referral benefits I have outlined above.

Some of you might be wondering what you just read. Why was it so difficult, until now, to come up with an easy solution to acquiring referrals? Why had you never heard or read about this amazing strategy that you will soon discover?

Great questions, and in the next chapters, we will explore the reasons why and give you an easy workable strategy you need to acquire these eight referrals or more.

Just let me say again that the strategy works because it mostly goes *against* conventional wisdom that many people follow. If this strategy followed acceptable ways of getting referrals, it would never have worked. More about this in the next chapter.

The strategy is very simple, but you do have to follow the steps, the dialogue, and the rationale outlined in the book. How easy it is will astonish you. The learning curve is very fast, and you can implement the strategy immediately after you finish reading the book.

People do business with you because they trust you. They have a good feeling about your sincerity and integrity. They feel you have their best interest at heart and really want to help them solve their problems.

I also sincerely believe they want to reciprocate and help you as well but do not know how to do it or what to do. This book will teach you how to get the referral help you want. It will also teach you how to make it very easy for your clients/customers to assist you in this task while feeling good about helping you.

To maximize your results with this system, it is also important to remember:

1. New clients prefer to meet you through a referral versus any other way.

2. Referrals are the most cost-effective method of building your business.

3. Lifetime value of a client is essential to your business—and part of that is your clients/customers referring new people to you over a lifetime.

4. You do not sell products and services; you sell solutions to problems.

5. To maximize your results, use an easy, workable system, like the one outlined in this book.

6. Your expectation is to get eight referrals or more from your prospects and clients/customers.

Because this is a unique referral system that produces immediately results. The next two chapters are essential to understand the whole strategy, followed by the special dialogs that make the strategy succeed almost every time.

2

PARADIGM SHIFT

The word *paradigm* comes from the Greek. It means "a model, theory, perception, or frame of reference." In the more general sense, it's the way we see the world in terms of perceiving and interpreting.

Thomas Kuhn introduced the term "paradigm shift" in his book *The Structure of Scientific Revolution.* Kuhn shows how almost every breakthrough is first a break from tradition—old ways of thinking and old paradigms.

In order for you to get eight referrals or more from most of your prospects or clients/customers on a consistent basis, a paradigm shift must occur in your way of thinking and how you view the transaction as a whole.

You will also need a different understanding of what is your main *goal* or *objective* when you interact with the prospect or client. If this paradigm shift does not happen and become internalized, you will continue to get referrals in a very random way, your business will suffer, and your production will look like a roller coaster over a given time frame. This often creates a great deal of stress.

The paradigm shift (what some call the "Aha!" experience) will probably not happen from reading a few of the hundreds of books that are available on the subject of referrals or any other marketing books. It also will not happen from listening to the so-called referral gurus or reading books written by theoreticians.

The traditional information about referrals in the old ways of thinking about the subject has been around for decades. The only difference today is that the old ideas are repackaged and marketed differently with the old paradigms.

Referrals, to remind you, are the most productive and efficient prospecting strategy. Referrals are the most cost-effective, compress the time to finalize the transaction, create larger sales, and are one of the best ways to expand your business rapidly.

The initial seeds of my paradigm shift occurred many years ago. I participated in our monthly lunch sales meeting. All I can remember is the location of the meeting and that there were about twenty people in the room. I don't remember the topic of the meeting or the speaker's name. But the meeting did have a huge impact on my future career as a small-business owner and a salesman.

I came out of the meeting thinking, "Aha!" in the form of a paradigm shift, knowing what it would take for me to stay in business and expand.

What happened in that meeting many years ago was as though a light were suddenly turned on inside me. A flash of unconventional wisdom struck me.

Like many of you, I was schooled in the old ways of thinking and conventional wisdom. But for as long as I can remember, many times I challenged conventional wisdom with simple questions like: "Is this the only way to do this?" "What if what most people think is impossible is possible?"

Or the title of this book: "Is it possible to get eight referrals or more every time I interact with prospects and clients/customers?"

So what was said in that meeting that caused me to have this amazing paradigm shift, this astonishing aha moment?

The speaker started the meeting with a very powerful question about the essence of the sale process. And the question was: *"What is your main objective, your main goal above all else, when you first interact with a prospect or client/customer?"*

Here are some of the answers he got:

- To make the sale/get the check.

- To build trust and friendship.

- To get the second appointment.

- To ask questions.

- To get to know my prospect and his concerns.

- To gather financial data and personal information.

- To probe for wants and needs and more.

What he did not hear was: REFERRALS! "Referrals," he said in an excited voice, "are your number-one objective and goal. Yes, referrals!"

And he continued, saying the reason why referrals are so important and *crucial* is that—if for some reason you do not finalize the transaction or make the sale, which will happen—at least you have new people to contact on a very favorable basis. That is absolutely huge!

His own answer to his question was the cause for my great aha and a huge "WOW!" I said to myself: "This is truly incredible and true!"

This was my first paradigm shift, a break from the old ways of thinking. It was followed by more paradigm shifts in my life, which enabled me to create this unique and powerful referral system you are about to discover.

In the years that followed, did I always keep this amazing referral message as a top priority every time I met a prospect or client? The answer is no, I did not. The reason is psychological barriers that we all have, which is also the subject of my next chapter.

Like many of you, because of the psychological barriers of obtaining referrals and the frustration it created, I implemented and tried many other marketing methods to acquire new clients over the years:

- cold calling
- seminars and workshops
- Internet leads

- direct mail
- purchasing leads
- advertising
- buying ads and more

What were my results, and how satisfied was I with those methods? I would say, looking back: poor, frustrating, expensive, and a feeling of false hope.

Did these efforts help me grow my business and stay in business? Yes, they did, but in a very minimal, time-consuming way and with a great outlay of money. I knew, since my great aha moment and without a doubt, that nothing can beat referrals as a strategy to acquire new customers and grow my business.

I tried to find an easy and workable referral strategy for years. It eluded me, but at last I found it, and today I am sharing it with you.

Part of the old paradigm that had to be changed or eliminated was the idea that you have to build trust/friendship over a long period of time to get referrals. You need to *earn* that trust over a month, a year, five years, twenty years, or who knows how long.

You also need, according to the so-called referral experts, to spend a lot of time, energy, and money developing that trust. And then, maybe you will get referrals. Does it really have to be that long? Do you really have to spend that much money and time?

My own experience over many years taught me that this was not the case and that there is no direct correlation between time passed and the referrals you get. It all has to do with the right, workable strategy you develop to get the referrals.

To prove my point, I'll take you back thirty years ago when I started my career in the financial-service business. Today I still have some of the clients I met thirty years ago. Their net worth was close to zero at the time we first met, and now some have a net worth in the millions.

With most of them, I had an annual personal meeting year after year and at least four phone conversations a year. I would say I did a good job staying in touch with them, keeping them updated, and delivering great value and service. I also, most of the time, asked for referrals year after year. The result? Many of them *never* gave me even one referral until I started using the strategy you will read about here. And then I started getting my eight or more referrals from them. I know that some of you reading this paragraph had the same frustrating experience when asking for referrals.

That feeling will end soon if you implement my amazing referral strategy.

My only regret is that I didn't have this referral strategy thirty years ago. I could have helped many more people increase their net worth substantially and become financially independent.

In his books, seminars, and speeches, Tony Robbins repeats the idea that changing your beliefs can happen in a moment. It can happen now, or it can happened ten years from now. You control when it will happen. The same is true for acquiring eight or more referrals. If you think it is a long, frustrating, and expensive process, you are right. If you think it can be done the first time you meet a prospect, you are right about that too.

So do not wait for some day to get eight referrals or more and count on conventional knowledge to do it for you. That day may never come. Get them now, with my proven strategy. It is a win-win situation for you and your clients.

The psychological barriers that I will cover in the next chapter were a constant negative factor in doing what I knew I had to do. These barriers will be an ongoing challenge to you as you take action to get eight referrals or more. So let's go over them.

3
PSYCHOLOGICAL BARRIERS

It is not easy to be a small-business owner or a salesperson. If it were easy, everyone would do it. There are five powerful constant psychological barriers that confront us almost every day, especially when it comes to the subject of referrals. They are:

- fear

- asking

- rejection

- transcending your limiting beliefs

- believing in yourself

PSYCHOLOGICAL BARRIERS

Fear

I've heard and read many times that the biggest fear people have is public speaking. I would say the biggest fear salespeople and business owners have is asking for referrals.

Most of us are aware that if we want to move forward, we are going to have to confront fear. Unfortunately, many salespeople let fear stop them from taking the action of asking for referrals.

Few of us, on the other hand, feel the fear but don't let it keep us from doing what we want or *have to do to get the results we want.* We have learned, as author Susan Jeffers suggests" to feel the fear and do it anyway". As Dale Carnegie said, "You can conquer almost any fear if you will only make up your mind to do so. Remember, fear doesn't exist anywhere except in the mind."

We have to acknowledge that fear exists but not let it keep us from doing the important task of getting referrals. Some salespeople will do anything to avoid the uncomfortable feeling of fear. If you are one of those people, you run an even greater risk of never getting the referrals you want and deserve and not getting the desired results. Taking risks is required to build a more successful and profitable business.

Today almost all our fears are self-created and, unfortunately, a constant emotional battle. We frighten ourselves by imagining negative outcomes of asking for referrals. Luckily, because we are the ones doing the fantasizing, we are also the ones who can stop the fear. Psychologists say that fear is **F**antasized **E**xperience **A**ppearing **R**eal.

So really, the keywords are: *I scare myself by imagining*. All fear is, again, self-created by imagining some negative outcome in the future, and we need to remember that.

So how do we overcome fear? One way is to stop and ask ourselves what we are imagining that is scary to us, and then replace those thoughts with images that are exactly the opposite. In the case of referrals, instead of imaging your prospect with a mean demeanor saying *no* to your request for referrals, imagine him having a big smile and a great passion and excitement to give you eight wonderful referrals.

You can also focus on the physical sensation you are feeling—the sensation you now associate with fear. Replace these emotions with feelings you would like to experience: calmness, courage, confidence, and happiness.

It is also a good idea to often remind yourself how many times you overcame fear in the past. I am sure many of you were reluctant to ask for referrals when you knew you should. Some of the time, somehow, you mustered the courage and asked for referrals, and you were surprised by how easy it was to get them. Do you remember those great feelings you had overcoming your fear?

Asking

Percy Ross said, "You've got to ask. Asking is, in my opinion, the world's most powerful and neglected secret to success and happiness."

So why are we afraid to ask for referrals? We are afraid of many things, such as looking needy, foolish, or stupid. But mostly, we fear rejection—hearing the dreaded word "*No.*" But what we are actually doing is rejecting ourselves in advance. We are saying no to referrals before anyone else even has a chance to say no.

Don't assume that you are going to get a no. Take the risk to ask for referrals. If they say no, you are no worse off than when you started. If they say yes, you are a lot better off.

The good news is that you will *get* the eight referrals or more in the majority of the time when you ask for them. Your level of confidence will soar. It will become so easy and natural to ask. After a short time, you will wonder why you were afraid to ask for referrals all these years.

When you ask, don't forget:

1. You want to be clear and specific—eight referrals or more and why.

2. Have the mind-set that you expect to get these referrals every time.

3. Assume you will get them *now*. Not a month, a year, or ten years from now or who knows when.

Rejection

If you are going to be successful, you are going to need to learn how to deal with rejection. Rejection is a natural part of life. To get over rejection, you have to realize that rejection is really a myth. It is simply a concept that you hold in your head. Think about it. If you ask for referrals from a prospect, and they say no, you did not have any referrals before you asked for them, and you do not have any after you asked for them. The situation didn't get worse; it stayed the same. It only gets worse if you tell yourself, "I can't handle this anymore. I don't want to hear no again. I've had it!"

The truth is, you never have anything to lose by asking for referrals, and if there is possibility for a huge gain, by all means ask. Whenever you ask for referrals or anything else, some people will say yes, and some will say no. So what! Continue asking.

Later in the book, you will discover the dialogue that will beat the rejection blues and allow you 90 percent success or better every time you ask for your eight referrals or more.

Transcending Your Limiting Beliefs

Many of us have beliefs that limit our success, especially when it comes to referrals. Moving beyond your limited belief is critical to succeeding in getting the eight referrals, or more, that you want. You can learn how to identify those beliefs and replace them with positive ones that support your goals.

As you read this book, I am sure some negative thoughts are rearing their ugly heads and telling you that you are not capable of getting eight referrals or more.

Where are these thoughts coming from? One is from early-childhood programming, when our parents, grandparents, and other adult role models repeatedly said, "No, no, no. It can't be done." They also stem from what you hear as an adult from peers and mentors and what you read about what can be done and what can't.

To accomplish what you want and transcend your limiting beliefs, you will need to take action as soon as you finish this book. You will then empower yourself to overcome this limited belief and achieve what you thought was impossible to do.

Believing in Yourself

If you are going to be successful in getting eight referrals or more, you have to believe that you can make it happen. You have to believe you have the right knowledge and information to be able to pull it off. You also need to have the self-confidence, self-assurance, and the deep-seated belief that you have what it takes to create your desired results.

Believing in yourself is a choice. It is an attitude you develop. You must choose to believe that you can get your eight referrals or more every time you meet a prospect or client/customer.

PSYCHOLOGICAL BARRIERS

If you assume and act *as if* it is possible to get eight referrals, then you will take the actions outlined in this book to create that result. If you are doubtful and convinced it is impossible, you will not take the necessary action, and you will not get the results. It, in a way, becomes a self-fulfilling prophecy.

To be successful in getting your eight referrals, you also have to let go of the words "I can't." This is probably the most destructive phrase in any language. The words *"I can't"* actually hurt you. They make you less secure when you state them or think about them.

More than that, you must take responsibility to remove the word "can't" from your vocabulary. It is very difficult, but it can be done.

Other destructive thoughts that need to be eliminated are: "I feel embarrassed asking for referrals." "My parents told me it's not right to beg for business." "I do not deserve referrals." These and similar thoughts are destructive.

The bottom line is that you need to detach yourself from your personal feelings of self-doubt and focus on the tremendous results and satisfaction you will achieve by implementing this amazing referral system.

4
THE INITIAL POSITIONING

THE INITIAL POSITIONING OF THE REFERRAL CONVERSATION is very crucial in achieving the outcome of gaining eight referrals or more, a majority of the time, from your prospects or clients/customers.

Forgetting, skipping, or fearing this step or not emphasizing it enough will make it much more difficult to stay on track and achieve your referral goals. And it will cost you in lost profits and sales.

First, let's talk about this initial conversation with new prospects you meet, and later we will discuss the conversation with existing clients/customers. What we are talking about here is the short conversation you *must* have about the way you get *compensated.* This dialogue must happen in your first meeting with the prospect.

I know that the readers of this book are all involved in different businesses, where the sales meeting from the initial meeting to getting the order and finalizing the sale could take anywhere from fifteen minutes to days, weeks, or even months. Some of you will have only one short meeting, some of you will have two meetings on different days, and some of you will have multiple meetings on different days.

It *does not* matter how many meetings it takes. What does matter is that the essential conversation about the way you get *compensated* must always happen at the first meeting.

Why is this conversation so important? Because, here, you will introduce and plant the seed of the importance of referrals to your business. Referrals, as you remember from the paradigm-shift chapter, are your number-one objective. Yes, it is your first priority when you meet prospects or clients/customers.

How and what you exactly say is up to you. I will give you some guidelines and share a dialogue to get the maximum impact. A very strong message for the prospect is that getting referrals is essential to your business and its survival, as well as your ability to deliver exceptional ongoing service to them.

As I said, somewhere in the first meeting, you must start a dialogue with them on how you get compensated. Be sure you go over it with them, whether it's by commission, hourly rate, flat fee, percentage of the gross sale, or any other method.

After the above dialogue, take a long pause, take a deep breath, and say the following. (Let's say the prospect's name is Mary McReferral.)

"Mary, my long-term goal and my purpose is to provide you with exceptional service. In order to achieve this, my business *has* to grow. As you probably know, it is not an easy task in today's world.

"Mary, of all the methods that are available to me to grow my business and give you the future service that you deserve, none of them can rival growing my business via referrals. None of them!

"In other words, Mary, my long-term compensation mostly comes from referrals. It is what has kept me in business for X years and will give me the ability to provide you and my other clients with outstanding service that you all expect. Does that make sense?"

At this point, if Mary has no questions, you say, "Great. We will come back to the subject of referrals later." Then you should immediately continue with your presentation, data gathering, or whatever your agenda is at the first meeting.

As for existing clients and customers, whenever you get together with them to introduce a new product, for an annual review, or for any other reason, you can skip the initial positioning that we just talked about.

THE INITIAL POSITIONING

You will go directly to the referral conversation in the next chapter. The dialogue you will have with them, after you finalized a new transaction or did not as you are finishing the meeting.

Next we will talk about the referral conversation that you will have with them. This conversation is the most important and significant dialogue you will have in achieving the outcome you are looking for. Do not skip any of the dialogues. Go over them enough times to say them naturally in your own words, where the dialogue will flow smoothly and with ease.

5
THE REFERRAL CONVERSATION

If you follow my guidelines and share the dialogue outlined here with your prospects or clients/customers, you will have tremendous success.

This dialogue is a must if you want to get the referral results you deserve. This conversation will be very challenging. The paradigm shift and the psychological barriers of fear, asking, rejection, transcending your limited beliefs, and believing in yourself will all come into play here.

When should this conversation take place? It should start immediately after you have finalized the transaction or made the sale.

If you did not succeed in making the sale, it is a judgment call. If you feel you built some rapport with the prospect and they appreciated your effort, then by all means, go ahead with the referral conversation. If you don't feel it, then just don't have it.

You could also ask him if the information he received was valuable. If he says yes, you could ask him another question. Is it possible that some of the people he knows could benefit from your products or services? If he says yes, go ahead with the referral conversation.

It does not matter if your sales meeting from the initial meeting to getting the order and finalizing the sale takes fifteen minutes, days, weeks, or even months. The conversation wills always take place after you made or did not make the sale.

Going forward with the referral conversation, at this point, after making the sale, is a tremendous challenge. Psychologically, you have a huge barrier to overcome, and here is why.

You have just finished the transaction, and you are now on a high. You're very excited. Your tendency and impulse, at this moment, is to run for the door: to pack your belongings, or go to the next appointment and thank the client, and disengage. Some of you will remember to ask, in a very weak and hesitant voice and with one foot out the door, for referrals: "Do you know anyone else who would benefit from my service/product?"

"No, not really. If I think of someone, I'll let you know." Or he says, "I don't give referrals until I know you better." And you answer, "OK," and then, "thanks," and the meeting is over, and you didn't get any referrals.

Or you may get similar responses that you have heard before when you ask for referrals. If you have been in sales or in business for even one month, you know what I am talking about.

Now, instead of rushing to finish the meeting and disengaging like you have always done after the sale, you now know that your moment of truth has arrived. You have to muster all the courage and strength that you have at this moment. You become very calm and totally relaxed, with a big smile on your face. You remember with clarity and passion that your main goal and objective is getting eight referrals or more. You believe that you can do it and remember that the meeting is not finished yet. And now it is just the beginning of the most exciting and challenging part of the meeting.

Part One

Now that the new you is relaxed and calm after the sale, your prospect is waiting for your next move. As you sincerely thank him for giving you the opportunity to serve him, you are also neatly stacking the paperwork you just completed and moving it to one of the table corners at the same time. As you are pushing the paperwork to the corner, you also reach out and pull out a *green* letter-size piece of paper that is positioned on the top of the stack.

On the top of the *green* sheet of paper, on both sides, is written **"REFERRAL FORM."** On the line below is written, "Your Name(s)," with a long line to the right of it. (This is for names of the prospects or clients.) Below that, on both sides and written eight times, is "Referred Name(s)" and below that "Phone Number," with a long line to the right. The eighth and last line of the referred names and phone numbers is positioned near the bottom of the page. (See Appendix I.)

Now, some of you are probably wondering why the referral form is *green*. One is to remind you of the color of money. But a more important reason is to distinguish it from any other paperwork you have and to remind you of its vital importance in getting your eight or more referrals *now*, before you part ways with your client.

Part Two

As you take out the green sheet, turn it around, and position it facing your client, Mary McReferral. Let her view the eight referrals on both sides of the sheet for about thirty seconds without saying a word.

(Go to www.eightreferrals.com to print your own green referral sheets.)

If you pay close attention to her facial expressions, you will notice that she is a little shocked. As if saying: "What? You want eight referrals from me?" And, "That's too much," or, "You're kidding, right?"

After the thirty seconds have passed, say, "Mary, do you remember our conversation in the beginning where I explained to you how I get compensated? And you remind her if it is by commission, hourly rate, flat fee, percentage of the gross sale, or any other method. And you wait for her answer of "Yes."

And you continue, reminding her the second way you get compensated is by referrals. Explain that, of *all* the methods available to you to grow your business and give her the future service that she deserve, none of them can rival growing your business via the referrals you receive. Do not continue the dialogue until you hear her saying, "Yes, I remember that," or, "Yes, I understand."

If you feel you need to make it clearer to her, you can repeat what you said in Chapter 4 about your long-term compensation mostly coming from referrals. It is what kept you in business for X years and what gave you the ability to provide your clients with the outstanding service they expect.

Part Three

As you continue, while very relaxed and confident and looking straight at her, say, "Mary, I understand that this it is a long list of referrals," as you move your head up and down in agreement with her.

As you continue and say the next paragraph, you want to be very clear and calm. Tell her, "This, however, is what I have found. Over the years, Mary, before I had the green referral sheet, when I asked for referrals from my new customers, these are the results I got:

"Half of them did give me referrals, and half of them did not. I truly believe that all of them wanted to help me if they felt and believed I provided them with excellent service. However, they did not know how to do it.

"From the half that did provide me with referrals, I got between one and three referrals. Rarely did I get any more. But once in a while, I did get more, but that happened very seldom."

Part Four

"What I also found out, Mary, if people gave me one to three referrals and less than eight, my chances of having a transaction with any of the referrals were very slim. If it happened, it was very rare.

"For example, let's say, Mary, you gave me the names of Bill, Lisa, and Beth as referrals. This is what happened most of the time.

"I called Bill first and said, 'Hi Bill, this is Reuven, and Mary McReferral told me to contact you.' And I explained my services. Bill answered, 'Thank you for calling, but I have an adviser and am happy with his services. Thank you for calling.' And the conversation was over.

"Then I called Lisa, your second referral, and said, 'Hi Lisa, this is Reuven, and Mary McReferral told me to contact you.' And I explained to her what I do. Lisa answered, 'Thank you for calling, but I just lost my job. Call me in a year. Thank you for calling.' And the conversation was over.

"I picked up the phone and called your third referral, Beth. 'Hi Beth, this is Reuven, and Mary McReferral told me to contact you." And I explained to her what I do. Beth answered, 'Thank you for calling, but I just got a wonderful new adviser, and I really like him. Thanks anyway for calling.' And the conversation was over."

Part Five

Over the years, I did have some successes with the one to three referrals that I got. But the sales were few and far between. One day I wised up and realized that I need to ask for more referrals and have a better strategy.

I set my goal to do business with at least one referral of those I got from my prospects or clients/customers. After playing with the number and my own experience, I figured it out. I needed to get at least eight referrals to achieve one sale. Next my question was: is it possible to do that? Can it really be done? Can I get eight referrals or more, a majority of the time, from my prospects or clients/customers?

I never heard or read anywhere in my many years in business about this impossible goal until I came up with the idea. I asked many people if it were possible, and they all answered, "Are you crazy?"

I knew, at that point, what my goal was: doing business with at least one referral from the eight I got. I told myself it would work because I would make it work. I had everything to gain and nothing to lose. So I went for the unattainable challenge and made it work after many trials and errors.

A note for readers: You are all in different businesses. Your goals are different. The quality of the referrals that you will get from implementing my system will be different as well. Some of you will build stronger rapport with prospects than others. The result will be that some of you will make more than one sale on average from eight referrals, and some of you will need to ask for more referrals to reach one sale. That is the reason the green referral sheet has eight names on both sides. (See Appendix I.)

Part Six

My conversation in part four about my past experience with one to three referrals and my green referral sheet still on the table in front of Mary gets her to think silently along these lines:

"Now, I know that if I want to help him with referrals, I need to give him at least eight referrals or none. He just told me that if I provide him with less than eight referrals, it will not help him very much." (Assuming here that she is very impressed and excited with the product or service just provided to her and she wants to help you as well.)

While she is thinking silently, continue, and say to her: "You see now, Mary, why it important to provide me with eight referrals or more if you want to help me? Is that clear?" (Wait for her to say, "Yes.")

And then continue: "Less than eight referrals will rarely give me a chance to get a new client and build my business so I can provide you and others with excellent ongoing service. Does that make sense to you?" Do not continue until she says, "Yes."

Part Seven

Now that Mary is in the process of internalizing the idea of providing you with eight referrals, you need to make it as easy as possible for her to take action and provide those referrals.

I call this next dialogue "The Random Process." It is a unique conversation that goes against the conventional wisdom that most of you were taught or read about. It will help you take a giant step forward in getting the eight or more referrals—and do it with great ease.

It will also help you eliminate the dreaded objection: "Let me think about who are the best candidates for your services and get back to you with their names." Sound familiar?

If you have been in sales for a while, you probably know that the chances of them getting back to you with a list of referrals is very slim or nonexistent. Why? I do not know, but I do know that that's the reality.

Part Eight

Now we will continue where we left off in part six. Ask Mary, while looking straight at her and with confidence: "Mary, *if* you gave me eight referrals, would you know for sure who from the eight will end up doing business with me?" Don't say a word, wait for her answer, and she will probably say, "No, I don't know."

"As you remember from what I said before, Mary, on average, I will do business with only one referral from the eight. In other words, Mary, who ends up doing business with me from the eight or more referrals you give me is anyone's guess. You do not know, and I certainly do not know. Is that correct?" Wait for her answer.

"Mary, what all this means is that I really do not care which eight referrals you provide to me. This is a random process and a numbers game. You might think you know who are the best referrals, but is it also possible that you don't know?" Wait for the answer. She will think for a second and then say that you are probably right.

This short dialogue is a great relief for Mary. Now she is telling herself: "I have about one hundred names and phone numbers stored in my phone/mobile device. This is cool. He is only asking for eight referrals, and he doesn't care which ones. Wow, that's easy! But I will still provide him with the names that I think will be his best prospects."

And she continues to think. "Yes, I have my phone/mobile device here with me. It will take me no time to write down the names on the green referral sheet." And you are one step closer to receiving the eight referrals or more with ease.

Part Nine

One more major concern that some clients will have is who contacts the referrals first after providing you with the names and phone numbers. Do you contact them first, or does the client? You must deal with this issue before the client brings it up.

Let's go back now to our dialogue with Mary. Now that we talked about the random process, Mary is more relaxed, and you can see a smile on her face.

"One more thing, Mary. Some clients, not all, want to contact the referrals they just provided to me before I contact them. They want to tell them that I will be contacting them and briefly explain, in their own words, what I do.

"In the past, Mary, I was all for it. I thought it was fair and the right thing to do. However, what I found out over many years is that it could do more harm than good. Let me explain.

"Mary, when someone who just did business with me contacts his referrals, his ability to explain what I do is limited. He will struggle with words and ideas as he tries to pass on the information. He will sound hesitant and uncertain. What the referred person will hear, usually, is a confused message. When that happens, in most cases, he will say he's not interested.

"Now contrast that, Mary, to when I call the referral. I am the professional, the expert, and I know my products/services. I can explain with more confidence what I do. If he has specific questions or concerns, I can address them with more clarity as well.

"My ability to communicate better than my client about my business at this important moment is crucial. It will give me a better chance to secure an appointment with him. Does this make sense, Mary?" Wait for her answer.

Part Ten

A note to readers: some clients will insist on contacting their clients before you do. Respect their wish. But try to get them to write down the eight referrals, if possible, on the green sheet in front of them. The reason is that, if you do not get the referrals names now, you will have a slim chance to get them later.

In this situation, if they give you the referrals and phone numbers, thank them, and ask how much time they will need to contact the referrals. If they say, for example, two weeks, ask them if it is OK for you to follow up and contact the referrals in three weeks.

Try to avoid contacting your new client directly and asking them if they talked to the referrals. My experience is that they rarely will take the action. It is better for you to contact the referral directly after the agreed time has passed, and ask if your new client talked to them about you and your services. If yes, great. If not, continue your conversation, and try to secure a meeting with them.

Part Eleven

Action time! This is the moment to take the action you waited for by asking your new client or prospect to write down the eight referrals or more.

The transition to this dialogue should be very natural and smooth. I know that the first few times you do it, you will feel very uncomfortable. You will feel scared and hesitant. So my recommendation is to practice it. The more you practice the dialogue before and in between meetings, the more confident you will become.

I know you will still feel the fear, but do not let it stop you. Each time you succeed in getting the referrals, your confidence will grow, and you will feel more comfortable. After a while, it will become very natural for you to ask for the referrals, and I dare to say you will start to enjoy it. In time, you will look forward to this fearful action.

Part Twelve

You are sitting across from Mary. You ask for the last time if she has any questions. If not, continue the dialogue.

"OK, Mary, you have the green referral sheet in front of you. Also, by the way, do you have the incredible electronic wonder device called cell phone/mobile device?"Yes it is my purse.

"Great". Here's a magic pen for you to write down the names and phone numbers."(Hand her the pen) In a smiling voice and shrugging your shoulders like you really do not care and continue.

"Again, Mary, I really do not care whose names you write down. As I told you before, this is a random process and a numbers game. You do not know and neither I, who are the best referrals, so any eight names or more will be fine"

Wait until she writes the first name. Absolutely do not say a word, even if the silence lasts for three minutes or more. At this point, she will start writing the names, or she will say something like, "I don't give out names."

If she says the above sentence, you go over the dialogue in the next part (part thirteen), paragraph four. Say to her that if you do business with one of her referrals, you will give her a small gift of appreciation. This is usually a gift certificate in X amount of dollars. That should motivate her to start writing the names of the referrals.

After she writes the first name and continues to look in her phone for the next name, say, "Mary, you probably have an idea who are the best referrals. It will help if you provide those names, but again, it does not matter." And let her continue searching for names and writing them on the referral sheet.

As she continues to writes the names and you feel that you have a good rapport with her. You can say, in a joking manner, "By the way, Mary, how many names and numbers are stored in your phone?" Let's say she tells you she has one hundred. You say, "Wow, that's great! So you might be able to help me even more and provide me with more than eight names. Couldn't you?"

After you ask the question, keep silent, and in many cases, you have just doubled the amount of referrals you are going to get.

Why? Now she is thinking and telling herself, "I have one hundred names. I can easily help him even more by providing him with more than eight random names now that I've started writing them down. Yes, why not write down another eight names on the other side of the green sheet?" Will this happen often? Yes, and more times than you think.

As I told you before, she will probably provide you with the referrals she thinks will be the most valuable to you. Remember, she wants to help you the best she can, and you made it very easy for her to do it.

Part Thirteen

When she finishes writing the names, thank her for the business and the kind referrals she gave you. As you thank her, slide the sheet toward you, and turn it around so that you can see the names and phone numbers of the referrals.

As you do it, say, "Mary, thank you again. We are almost finished. Just a few quick questions."

You now want Mary to give you brief but important information on the referrals that is relevant to your business. You are all in different businesses. If age is relevant, ask her. If profession is important, ask her. Ask if the referrals are coworkers or how she knows them, as well as any other relevant questions. As she provides you with the information on each referral, write it down on the green sheet next to their names.

When you are finished, again say, "Mary, thank you. I really appreciate your kind help. This is what I will do for you. If I do business with your referrals, I will call you and let you know whom I did business with.

I would also like to give you, at the same time, a small gift. It's not much. It is, again, just to let you know how much I appreciate your kindness and help. For every referral that does business, I will give you a gift certificate for X amount of dollars to your favorite restaurant or store. Again, thank you, Mary. Any questions?"

If she has no questions at this point, this ends your meeting.

Good luck. This referral system will work for you and take your business to a new level—if you follow the steps outlined in this book and take action.

6

EASIER TO GET STARTED

I HOPE BY NOW THAT YOU REALIZE HOW POWERFUL THIS system is to obtain eight referrals or more—and getting those, most of the time, from very prospect or client/customer.

This chapter will make it even easier on you to use this amazing referral system to grow your business. I wrote this chapter as a quick reference and a summary reminder of the dialogues you need to have with your prospects or clients/customers. (*I would suggest printing this chapter.*)

I recommend you read these chapter dialogue summaries before every appointment until you are totally confident that you have internalized the dialogue steps.

The dialogue reminders that follow are summaries of the previous chapter dialogues ("The referral Conversation") that start after you made or did not make the sale. These are the most important dialogues of the whole system to produce the results of getting eight referrals or more.

To print this chapter, go to www.eightreferrals.com.

Remember

- **These dialogues are a must if you want to get the referral results you deserve.**

- **The dialogues should start immediately after you have or haven't made the sale.**

- **After making the sale or not making the sale, it's a tremendous mental challenge to continue the dialogue, but do it!**

- **You now know that your moment of truth has arrived. You should muster all the courage you have to produce the results.**

- **You have to believe that you can do it.**

- **Clients/customers want to help you. They just don't know what to do or how to do it.**

Reminder Number One

1. Show the client/customer both sides of the green referral sheet (see Appendix I). Let them look at it for thirty seconds. Agree that it is a lot of names.

2. Remind them how you get compensated, including referrals. Emphasize referrals.

3. Explain why the green sheet has eight names. Why? Half of the people will only give you one to three referrals. The other half will give you none.

4. Their now thinking: "I need to give him eight referrals or more or none."

Reminder Number Two

1. Explain that from the eight referrals you get, you will only make one sale on average (use a different number for your business if need to).

2. Ask: "Do you know for sure, from the eight referrals you give me, who will end up doing business with me?" The answer, obviously, is no. Wait for their answer.

3. What all this means is that you do not care which eight referrals they provide to you. It is a random process and a numbers game.

4. Their thinking now is: "I have about eighty names stored in my phone/mobile device. He is only asking for eight referrals, and he doesn't care which ones. Wow, that should be easy!"

Reminder Number Three

1. It is very important for you to bring this up: who contacts the referral first?

2. You do. Why? You are the expert—the professional. You have much better knowledge of your products/services.

3. Only you can answer specific questions or concerns that the referral may have.

4. Your ability to communicate better than your client about your business at this crucial moment will give you a better chance to secure an appointment.

Reminder Number Four

1. Action time! The moment of truth has arrived! Ask your new client or prospect to write down the eight referrals or more.

2. The transition to the request must be very natural (like it's no big deal). You will feel uncomfortable and fearful, but do not let it stop you from asking.

3. Remind them of the electronic marvel they have—a cell phone/mobile device. Ask if they have it with them. (Most will have it.)

4. As they get the phone, remind them that you really do not care whose names they write down. It is a random process and a numbers game.

5. Hand them a pen with which to write. Absolutely do not say a word until they write down the first referral.

6. After they write down three or four referrals, ask jokingly how many names and numbers are stored in their phone.

7. If it is a large number (more than fifty), there is a good chance that they will provide you with more than eight names. Ask for more.

Reminder Number Five

1. When they complete writing the referral names, thank them for the business and the referrals.

2. Tell them that you are almost finished, and then ask them a few quick questions relevant to your business about each referral. Write the answers on the green sheet.

3. Again, let them know how much you appreciate their business and the referrals. Let

them know that for every referral that does business with you, you will give them with a gift certificate for X amount of dollars to their favorite restaurant or store.

APPENDIX I

Referral Form

1. Your Name(s) _____

    Referred Name(s) _____

    Home Phone_____ **cell Phone**_____

    Your Name(s) _____

    Referred Name(s) _____

    Home Phone_____ **cell Phone**_____

    Your Name(s) _____

    Referred Name(s) _____

    Home Phone_____ **cell Phone**_____

APPENDIX I

Your Name(s) _____

Referred Name(s) _____

Home Phone_____ **cell Phone**_____

Your Name(s) _____

Referred Name(s) _____

Home Phone_____ **cell Phone**_____

Your Name(s) _____

Referred Name(s) _____

Home Phone_____ **cell Phone**_____

Your Name(s) _____

Referred Name(s) _____

Home Phone_____ **cell Phone**_____

Your Name(s) _____

Referred Name(s) _____

Home Phone_____ **cell Phone**_____

**To print a copy of this referral form go to
www.eightreferral.com**

APPENDIX II

This is an example of a first phone follow-up conversation (you should customize it to your business).

[Name?]

Hi, I'm [your name].

Do you have a minute?

You don't know me, but we have a mutual friend. Does [XXX's—the person who referred them to you] name ring a bell? Do you know him or her?

Anyhow, I promised him/her that I would give you a call. <u>And let me tell you why he/she wanted me to call.</u>

I did some business with them, and they were very pleased.

<u>So let me tell you what I do.</u>

APPENDIX II

<u>I work with people that want to improve their financial situation NOW and achieve financial independence.</u>

I have been doing this for [X] years and have hundreds of satisfied clients.

<u>Here are some of the areas in which I can help you. I can...</u>

- save you money on taxes and put it back into your budget;

- help you build a solid emergency fund to protect you from future job loss, medical emergency, car problems, and other emergencies;

- provide strategies for early and comfortable retirement;

- help you minimize your debt or get rid of it all together;

- help you avoid risky investment and protect your family;

- make sure that your financial decisions create opportunities for you, not for others; and

- provide strategies on how to beat the banks, the government, and investment companies in the game of trying to make you poorer.

These financial strategies to help you are available to anyone, but many people are too busy to learn about them, take advantage of them, and take a giant step toward a better financial future.

<u>So, what I'd like to do at their request</u> is set up a time when we can get together and discuss if these ideas could help you as well.

I am very confident that one hour with me will be one of the best investments you can make in yourself, your future, and your family's future.

Now, when we get together, you can't buy anything, so put your checkbook away. I can see you [date/time] or [date/time]. What's going to work best for you?

To print a copy go to www.eightreferrals.com.

ABOUT THE AUTHOR

Reuven Shuval has been in the financial-service business for thirty years and has hundreds of satisfied clients. He is also a financial educator who has conducted many financial seminars and workshops for small and large corporations. He lives with his wife, Natalia, in Hillsboro, Oregon.

Over the past three decades, as a small-business owner, Reuven was very frustrated with the advice he got regarding referrals from books, experts, and other sources.

What was missing was a proven, simple, workable referral strategy that is also *quantifiable*. One that costs you very little, is not time-consuming, and can be executed immediately.

It took Reuven years to figure it out, but in the end, he achieved his goal of getting eight referrals or more and obtaining them, most of the time, from *every* prospect or client/customer. And now, in this book, he is sharing this amazing and easy strategy with you.

www.ingramcontent.com/pod-product-compliance
Lightning Source LLC
Chambersburg PA
CBHW071806170526
45167CB00003B/1187